Backyard Ducks

A year of life at home with Pekin ducks

words, photos, and art by Yvonne Blacker

Dedicated to our Pekin ducks who kept us company while staying at home, and to my family who helped raise them.

- photos taken March 2020 to March 2021 -

Summary: Seven baby Pekin ducks are brought home by a New England family at the start of the pandemic to keep them company while "staying at home." Original photos capture the joy of raising them from duckling stage to maturity.

ISBN 979-8-9853878-2-7

1. Ducks - Non Fiction 2. Farm Animals - Non Fiction 3. Pet Ducks - Non Fiction

There is a lot to know about raising baby ducks. First of all, they are super fun to watch. And they are also very cute. And even a little bit silly. This storybook shares what our family learned in our first year of raising seven Pekin ducks.

- Yvonne Blacker, author

Baby Pekin ducks weigh less than one pound.

Full grown
Pekin ducks
weigh about
ten pounds.

Baby ducks need lots of fresh water and pellets.

Baby ducks stay cozy by sleeping in a pile.

Baby ducks like to have a best friend nearby.

Ducks like to get their feet wet.

When they get older, they love to dive under the water.

Ducks need to preen themselves every day.

Ducks dig
in the mud
for bugs with
their beaks.

Then it's bath
time again.

Ducks will
wait for their
humans to
return with
a treat like
frozen peas.

Ducks clean
their beaks
by sticking
their head
under water.

A quick dip
can help
get those
feathers out.

Ducks like to
hide together
in the shade.

Ducks like to eat lots of healthy snacks.

Ducks like
to eat chives
straight from
the garden.

Ducks like
to nibble on
rose petals.

Sometimes a
duck needs
a time out.

The yolk in a duck egg is bigger than the yolk in a chicken egg.

Ducks love rain and they don't mind the cold, but ducks don't love ice or deep snow.

Or cats.
Or foxes.
Or hawks.

Ducks wings
are strong.

Ducks drop their feathers or "molt." New feathers grow back to replace the old ones.

Pekin ducks can't fly, but they still go places.

Ducks get
tucked into
bed every
single night.

"Quack, quack, quack." Ducks like stories.

Want more duck stories?

Scan this code with a smart phone
for online access to duck videos,
coloring pages, and more!

www.ingramcontent.com/pod-product-compliance
Lightning Source LLC
Chambersburg PA
CBHW061143030426
42335CB00002B/89